Tom had invited his friend Megan for lunch. They were going to have pizza. It was his favourite food. Before they tucked into it, Tom's mum said a prayer, called a grace.

"Thank you, Lord, for this food and for our friends. Amen."

CW01651951

After lunch they went to visit Tom's church. They are both Christians, but Tom goes to St Mary's Anglican Church and Megan goes to King Street Baptist Church.

Tom's church is very old. Megan was amazed by the ceiling. It reminded her of an upside-down boat. Tom said that this part of the church was called the nave, a very old word meaning 'ship'. All along the nave were wooden seats called pews. Megan thought they would be hard to sit on!

Megan said that her church was very modern and a different shape. It had lots of chairs with cushions on. Tom thought that they sounded more comfortable!

Jesus
King of Kings

They went to look at the font. Tom described how his baby sister was baptised here. "The minister poured water on her head and made the sign of the cross on her forehead."

Tom told Megan that the font was near the entrance of the church to welcome people into the Christian family when they are baptised.

Megan said that her church had a small pool at the front, called a baptistery. "People are baptised when they are grown up," she explained, "and they are ducked right under water!"

The children went over to a large stained-glass window. Megan thought it was beautiful and noticed that it had lots of pictures of Jesus. The children spotted a picture of Mary and Joseph and the baby Jesus. Then they saw a picture of fishermen in a boat. "That's another boat!" Tom exclaimed. They each saw a different story in the window.

"In my church," Megan said, "we have lots of lovely banners hanging from the ceiling. They help people think about God and Jesus." Her favourite was the one that had a shining crown on it and the words 'Jesus is the King of Kings'. Tom thought the banners sounded lovely.

Jesus
King of Kings

On one side of the church they noticed someone standing quietly and lighting a candle. Tom explained that people did this when they had something special to pray for. Megan thought that was a good thing to do. They wondered what the person might be praying about.

Megan told Tom that in her church they had a worship band, which played in services. She liked the lively songs. "Sometimes we sing some children's songs," she added.

At the other side of the church was a noticeboard. Megan noticed the advert for Beavers and Cubs. "I go to a group called Explorers at my church," she said. "We do lots of fun things and have stories from the Bible."

Megan saw an advert for the church Fairtrade stall. Tom pointed out the 'Africa Project' poster. He told her that they had been raising money for a new school in Africa. Megan said that her church had a lunchtime club for elderly people.

They read about some of the other things that were happening.

Prayer and Study Group meets every Tuesday at 8.00 pm in the Vicarage
Fair Trade Stall
Open Every Saturday at the Coffee Morning 10 am – 12 pm
Cubs
Beavers
MEET WEDNESDAYS AT 5.30 PM & 6.00 PM
HELP AFRICA
WE NEED TO RAISE £10,000 TO HELP BUILD A SCHOOL
JUNIOR CHURCH every Sunday Morning for all Children
PARISH LUNCH
NEXT WEDNESDAY ALL ARE WELCOME

At the front of the church the children noticed there were two stands. Tom knew what these were. "That is the pulpit where the vicar stands to tell people about God and Jesus," he pointed. "And that one is the lectern." They looked at the big Bible that was resting on it. Megan found the eagle shape interesting. Tom explained that the wings were to remind people that God's love was to be spread all over the world.

Megan said that in her church they had a modern pulpit where the pastor preached from the Bible.

Then the children went to look at the altar. It had a beautiful tapestry on the front showing a cross, a dove and flames. These are all special Christian symbols.

Tom described how Christians kneel there and are given bread and wine to remember the last meal Jesus had with his friends. This is called Holy Communion.

Megan said that in her church they called it the Lord's Supper. "We have the wine in little glasses and we stay in our seats to share communion," she added.

Megan enjoyed her visit to Tom's church.
She asked Tom to come and visit
her church some time.

On her way home Megan tried
to remember all the different
things she had seen.

How many different
things can you remember?

Published by RMEP (Religious and Moral Education Press)
An imprint of Hymns Ancient and Modern Ltd (a registered charity)
St Mary's Works, St Mary's Plain, Norwich, Norfolk NR3 3BH

First published 2009

The Beaver and Cub logos on page 11 are Trademarks of the Scout Association and used by permission.

The Fairtrade mark on page 11 is used by permission. See www.fairtrade.org.uk and look out for this mark on products when you go shopping.

ISBN 978-1-85175-375-8

Designed and typeset by Topics – The Creative Partnership, Exeter
Printed in Great Britain by Halston & Co. Ltd, Amersham, Bucks